GOD SPEAKS
—YOUR—

LANGUAGE®

WORKBOOK

GOD SPEAKS
— YOUR —
LOVE
LANGUAGE®

#1 *NEW YORK TIMES* BESTSELLER
Gary Chapman
with Randy Southern

WORKBOOK

NORTHFIELD PUBLISHING
CHICAGO

Developed with the assistance of Peachtree Publishing Services
    (www.peachtreeeditorial.com). Special thanks to Randy Southern.
Interior design: Erik M. Peterson
Cover design: Faceout Studio, Jeff Miller
Cover graphic of bokeh copyright © 2024 by Ole moda/Shutterstock (1469341238).
    All rights reserved.
Cover graphic of gradient background copyright © 2024 by pungkas dika/
    Shutterstock (2252133041). All rights reserved.

ISBN: 978-0-8024-3299-5

We hope you enjoy this book from Northfield Publishing. Our goal is to provide high-quality, thought-provoking books and products that connect truth to your real needs and challenges. For more information on other books and products that will help you with all your important relationships, go to northfieldpublishing.com or write to:

Northfield Publishing
820 N. LaSalle Boulevard
Chicago, IL 60610

1 3 5 7 9 10 8 6 4 2

Printed in the United States of America

CONTENTS

INTRODUCTION

WELCOME to a labor of love.

The ten lessons in this book were created for one purpose: to strengthen and deepen your loving relationship with God. The process won't be easy. Nothing worthwhile ever is. This study will pose some challenging questions. It will take you outside your comfort zone. It will even require you to do homework.

But this isn't busywork. These lessons give you workable strategies for applying the principles of *God Speaks Your Love Language*. They offer glimpses of your spiritual potential when you harness the power of love languages.

If you're working through this study alone, take heart. Your solo efforts will likely have a profound impact on your relationship with God. Throughout *God Speaks Your Love Language*, you'll find accounts of difficult challenges that were overcome by one person's commitment to maximizing his or her use of love languages.

If you're working through this study as a couple, let patience, grace, and humor be your companions. Learning a new love language can be difficult, and there's more than a little trial and error involved. Show your appreciation for each other's efforts to communicate love to God and others in new and meaningful ways, no matter how clumsy those efforts are at first. And be sure to celebrate when those efforts hit the mark.

If you're working through this study in a group, pay attention to what your fellow group members share. Inspiration and wisdom can be found in unexpected places. In your interactions with fellow group members, be generous with your encouragement and sparing with your criticism. Ask appropriate follow-up questions to show your interest in their success.

Regardless of how you approach this study, you should be aware that the lessons in this book will require a significant investment of time and effort. There's a lot of important material in these pages. But it's virtually a risk-free investment. You will see dividends. And the more of yourself you pour into this workbook, the greater your dividends will be.

Enjoy the journey!

GARY CHAPMAN

OBJECTIVE

In reading this chapter, you will learn how the five love languages impact every relationship in your life, including your relationship with God.

UNDERSTANDING THE FIVE LOVE LANGUAGES

INSTRUCTIONS: Complete this first lesson after reading chapter 1 ("Understanding the Five Love Languages," pp. 19–29) of *God Speaks Your Love Language*.

KEY TERMS

Love languages: five distinct methods people use to communicate and receive emotional love.

Love tank: the emotional reservoir inside everyone that is filled when people speak to us in our primary love language.

OPENING QUESTIONS

1. Dr. Chapman introduces the five different love languages: words of affirmation, quality time, gifts, acts of service, and physical touch. Which love languages did your parents speak to you when you were a child? Which one, if any, made you feel especially loved? Explain. In retrospect, which love language would you have preferred they use?

2. When have you spoken the wrong love language to someone? Why did you choose to speak in that love language? What were the results? What did you take away from the experience?

THINK ABOUT IT

3. Dr. Chapman points out, **"There are thousands of ways to express verbal affirmation."** Of the examples he lists, which one is closest to the type of verbal affirmation you might offer a loved one? In what areas do you usually focus when you offer words of affirmation? Explain. If you were on the receiving end of the verbal affirmation, which one would be most meaningful to you? Explain.

4. Dr. Chapman suggests ideas for quality time with a small child, with your spouse, with a teenager, and with a single adult. What do they all have in common? What is the key to making quality time meaningful in each situation?

5. **"Gifts need not be expensive."** These words of Dr. Chapman make it clear that anyone can afford to be a gift giver. How can an inexpensive gift have a powerful impact on someone? When have you seen that played out in real life?

6. Dr. Chapman offers several examples of acts of service. Which ones are you capable of doing? What other ideas would you add to the list? Which acts of service would be especially meaningful to your loved ones?

7. What example does Dr. Chapman offer to illustrate the emotional power of physical touch? Why is it important for parents to find new dialects of physical touch when their children become teenagers? What types of physical touch would be most meaningful to your loved ones at this point in their lives?

8. How is a person's "love tank" like a car's gas tank? How can you tell when someone's love tank is empty? What is the key to making sure that your spouse, children, or parents feel loved?

9. Dr. Chapman writes, **"It is my premise that the love languages observed in human relationships all reflect various aspects of divine love."** With that in mind, which love language does God speak? Why is that important to understand?

TAKE IT HOME

Speaking the wrong love language can make you feel distant from the people closest to you. It can also make you feel distant from God. Speaking the right love language, on the other hand, can bring you extremely close to Him. That explains why all of us experience "valley" and "mountaintop" moments in our relationship with Him. On the left side of the line below, describe a valley experience—a time when God's love seemed distant to you. On the right side, describe a mountaintop experience—a time when God and His love seemed very near to you.

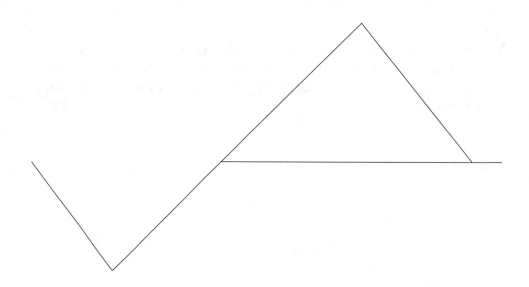

ABOUT THE LOVE LANGUAGES

Rate the following expressions of love according to how meaningful they would be to you, with 5 being the most meaningful and 1 the least meaningful. The results should give you an idea of what your primary love language is.

_____ You overhear a loved one telling someone how amazingly creative you are. (Words of Affirmation)

_____ A loved one cancels his or her plans in order to spend the day with you before you leave for a weeklong trip. (Quality Time)

_____ A loved one gives you a framed photo of the two of you taken during one of your very best days together. (Gifts)

_____ A loved one spends an entire Saturday afternoon cleaning your car, inside and out. (Acts of Service)

_____ A loved one gives you an impromptu back rub. (Physical Touch)

LOVE CHALLENGE

If you're new to the concept of love languages—and even if you aren't—you'll likely realize that you've been speaking the wrong love language to people you care about. As a result, they may not be aware of how much you love them. What steps can you take this week to change that?

STEP 1

STEP 2

STEP 3

STEP 4

STEP 5

STEP 6

Use this space for more notes, quotes, or lessons learned from the chapter.

OBJECTIVE

In reading this chapter, you will learn how God uses words of affirmation to communicate His love to and build relationships with people whose primary love language is words of affirmation—and how those people can, in turn, show love to others through verbal and written expressions.

GOD SPEAKS LOVE LANGUAGE #1: WORDS OF AFFIRMATION

INSTRUCTIONS: Complete this second lesson after reading chapter 2 ("God Speaks Love Language #1: Words of Affirmation," pp. 31–47) of *God Speaks Your Love Language.*

KEY TERM

Words of affirmation: verbal and written expressions of affection, appreciation, and encouragement that communicate love in profound ways for people who understand that love language.

OPENING QUESTIONS

1. Mark Twain once wrote, "I can live for two months on a good compliment." What compliment or word of praise still makes you feel good about yourself? Who said it? What were the circumstances? Why did it have such an impact on you?

2. What words of affirmation in the Bible are especially meaningful to you? Which passages do you turn to—or recite to yourself—when you need a boost in confidence? Explain.

THINK ABOUT IT

3. Dr. Chapman's story of Reuben and Gabrielle shows that speaking one love language fluently, as Reuben did, doesn't guarantee that the other person will feel especially loved. Gabrielle needed something else. When have you experienced a similar situation in your own relationships—or seen it played out in someone else's? What impact did the miscommunication have on the relationships?

4. After sharing the story of his conversion to Christ with Dr. Chapman, Reuben explained, **"I feel closest to God when I'm preaching."** His primary love language was words of affirmation. When do you feel closest to God? Explain.

5. According to Dr. Chapman, **"The way people interrelate on a human level tends to be true on a spiritual level as well."** What method did God use to get through to Reuben when he was **"a wandering college freshman"**?

6. Dr. Chapman writes, **"All the specific commands of God in both the Old and New Testaments affirm our worth, flow from His love, and direct us toward a higher goal. Some people find the commands of God restrictive and rebel against them."** On the other hand, what do those who know God believe?

7. As a young monk, Martin Luther tried hard to please God by following a life of discipline. How did the words of Romans 1:17 not only open his eyes to a better approach but also reveal his primary love language?

8. What evidence can you find in the writings of David, the second king of Israel, that suggests that his primary love language was words of affirmation?

9. Dr. Chapman talks about his conversation with Jason, a man who acknowledged that his love language is words of affirmation. How did Jason reply when Dr. Chapman asked him when he felt closest to God?

TAKE IT HOME

Here are a few passages that contain words of affirmation from the Bible. For each passage, describe a real-life scenario in which those words of affirmation could make you feel closer to God. For example, if you were questioning your self-worth, the words of Genesis 1:27 could remind you that God sees you as extremely valuable because you're created in His image.

"So God created man in his own image, in the image of God he created them; male and female he created them" (Genesis 1:27).

"Do not fear, for I am with you; do not be dismayed, for I am your God. I will strengthen you and help you; I will uphold you with my righteous right hand" (Isaiah 41:10).

"I will turn their mourning into gladness; I will give them comfort and joy instead of sorrow" (Jeremiah 31:13).

"Very truly I tell you, whoever hears my word and believes him who sent me has eternal life and will not be judged but has crossed over from death to life" (John 5:24).

DRAWING CLOSER TO GOD THROUGH WORDS OF AFFIRMATION

As Dr. Chapman's friend Jason pointed out at the end of the chapter, using words of affirmation in prayer can make us feel close to God. Gathering the material you need for such prayers is as easy as noticing and appreciating God's countless praiseworthy qualities. On the fruit tree below, identify various characteristics, gifts, and skills that God possesses. These are areas that are ripe for words of affirmation. You can start with the low-hanging fruit—the easy ones. These are characteristics that are obvious to most people—a list that might include His creativity, His power, and His love. The upper branches of the tree are the qualities of God that many people may not see or appreciate—a list that might include His holiness, His justice, and His discipline.

LOVE CHALLENGE

Who do you know who needs to hear words of affirmation this week? Which words do you think would be especially meaningful? What steps will you take to reach out to that person this week?

STEP 1

STEP 2

STEP 3

STEP 4

STEP 5

STEP 6

Use this space for more notes, quotes, or lessons learned from the chapter.

OBJECTIVE

In reading this chapter, you will learn how God uses quality time
to communicate His love to and build relationships with people whose
primary love language is quality time—and how those people can, in turn,
show love to others by spending meaningful, focused time with them.

GOD SPEAKS LOVE LANGUAGE #2: QUALITY TIME

INSTRUCTIONS: Complete this third lesson after reading chapter 3 ("God Speaks Love Language #2: Quality Time," pp. 49–59) of *God Speaks Your Love Language.*

KEY TERM

Quality time: a love language through which people experience emotional wholeness by spending purposeful time with, and enjoying the full attention of, someone else.

OPENING QUESTIONS

1. How would you describe the difference between spending time with someone and spending quality time with someone? When was the last time you spent quality time with someone? How did you ensure that your time together was quality?

2. When was the last time you spent quality time with God? What was your motivation for making that time happen? How did you ensure that your time together was quality? What did you take away from the experience?

THINK ABOUT IT

3. Dr. Chapman shares the story of Greta and Kevin, a married couple who encountered God powerfully in two very different ways. With their story in mind, how would you respond to someone who claimed that certain experiences with God are more valid than others? Why is it important to be respectful of—and curious about—other people's experiences with God?

4. What did quality time with God look like for Adam and Eve? What did quality time with God look like for Abraham? What do these biblical stories reveal about God and His interactions with His people?

5. The psalmist wrote, "The LORD is righteous in all his ways and faithful in all he does. The LORD is near to all who call on him, to all who call on him in truth" (Psalm 145:17–18). What can cause us to lose sight of His nearness—and the opportunities for quality time that come with it? What else did the psalmist and prophets say about quality time with God?

6. Dr. Chapman writes, **"The design of Jesus' earthly ministry was an illustration of quality time."** Given the demands on His time during His ministry, how was Jesus able to devote quality time to people? What is the takeaway for those who wish to follow His example?

7. Dr. Chapman shares the New Testament story of Jesus' visit to the home of Martha and Mary. How did Martha react to being in the presence of Jesus? How did Mary react? What can you conclude about their primary love languages based on their reactions? How did Jesus respond when Martha complained about Mary? Why is it important to consider other people's primary love languages before we weigh in on their relationship with the Lord?

8. Dr. Chapman tells the remarkable story of George Mueller, the nineteenth-century German minister who devoted his life to serving God and His people. What did quality time with God look like in George Mueller's life? What can you take away from his experience to deepen your own quality time with God?

9. How does it make you feel to know that God is ready and willing to meet you anytime, anywhere? How often do you take Him up on His offer?

TAKE IT HOME

One theme that runs throughout the chapter is that any time can be quality time with God if you want it to be. He will meet you anywhere, for as long as you like. With that in mind, how might you turn the following situations into quality time with God? What would you need to do during each situation to draw closer to Him?

Your morning commute

A long hike

Household tasks

Your bedtime routine

QUALITY TIME IN ACTION

Quality time isn't measured in length; it's measured in depth. Ten minutes of truly focused time can be more meaningful than an entire day of simply being in someone else's presence. With that in mind, how can you use quality time to communicate God's love to the following people?

A homeless person you pass on your way to work

A socially awkward coworker

A friend who's struggling emotionally

An elderly neighbor

LOVE CHALLENGE

You have twenty-four hours a day, seven days a week, to work with. How much of that time will you set aside for quality time with God this week? How much will you set aside for quality time with others? What steps will you take to make your quality time allotment a reality?

STEP 1

STEP 2

STEP 3

STEP 4

STEP 5

STEP 6

Use this space for more notes, quotes, or lessons learned from the chapter.

OBJECTIVE

In reading this chapter, you will learn how God uses gifts to
communicate His love to and build relationships with people
whose primary love language is gifts—and how those people can,
in turn, show love to others by giving them meaningful presents.

GOD SPEAKS LOVE LANGUAGE #3: GIFTS

INSTRUCTIONS: Complete this fourth lesson after reading chapter 4 ("God Speaks Love Language #3: Gifts," pp. 61–77) of *God Speaks Your Love Language.*

KEY TERM

Gifts: a love language in which a person experiences emotional wholeness through meaningful, well-chosen presents.

OPENING QUESTIONS

1. Describe a gift you received that proved the old saying "It's the thought that counts." Who gave you the gift? What made it so special? What were the circumstances? How did the person know the gift would be meaningful to you? How did you respond? What did you take away from the experience?

2. What's the best gift you've ever given someone? What were the circumstances? How did you know what to get? How did the recipient of your gift react? How did you feel? What did you take away from the experience?

THINK ABOUT IT

3. Anne Wenger and R. G. LeTourneau had profoundly different life experiences. Why does Dr. Chapman mention them together at the beginning of the chapter? What similarities do you see in their priorities and their attitude toward God's gifts?

4. What does the first chapter of God's Word tell us about His gift giving? What does the last chapter of His Word tell us? What does His relationship with Israel tell us? What does His interaction with Solomon tell us?

5. Dr. Chapman writes, **"The teachings of Jesus were permeated with the concept that God wants to give good gifts to those who love Him."** How did Jesus say those gifts would be distributed after His death, resurrection, and return to His Father in heaven? What did Jesus want His followers to know about God's gifts?

6. The New Testament writer James said, "Every good and perfect gift is from above, coming down from the Father of the heavenly lights, who does not change like shifting shadows" (James 1:17). His fellow writer John wrote, "See what great love the Father has lavished on us, that we should be called children of God!" (1 John 3:1). What material things does God give those who are faithful to Him? What spiritual things does He give us?

7. Dr. Chapman shares the compelling story of Monica, who turned her life around in a Teen Challenge program. What was Monica's experience with God's amazing gift giving? What was her experience with the gift giving of God's people? How did Monica incorporate gift giving into her interactions with other people? What is the takeaway for someone whose experiences are not as dramatic as Monica's?

8. What are some gifts from God that are given to everyone? What did the psalmist say about such gifts? Why is it hard for some people to recognize those things as God's gifts? What are some gifts from God that are reserved for those who ask? What did Jesus say about such gifts? What keeps some people from asking for them?

9. Dr. Chapman emphasizes, **"Requesting material things simply for the sake of possessing them is foreign to the biblical concept of love."** What happens when well-meaning people lose sight of that truth? What do sincere followers of Jesus always ask?

TAKE IT HOME

God's generosity knows no bounds. His gift giving never stops. No matter how many things we thank Him for, there are countless others we *could* thank Him for. Think about the last time you prayed. What did you thank God for? Which of His gifts did you single out for special mention? Write them in the first column below. Which gifts will you thank Him for the next time you pray? Write them in the second column.

IN MY LAST PRAYER, I THANKED GOD FOR . . .	IN MY NEXT PRAYER, I'LL THANK GOD FOR . . .

How can you keep track of the many new things to thank Him for every day?

FROM GIFT RECIPIENT TO GIFT GIVER

Dr. Chapman writes, **"We receive the gifts of wisdom, insight, experience, expertise, and material possessions to enrich the lives of other people."** How can you use the following gifts to enrich others? Let's take money, for example. If you know the cost of your church's youth retreat is $175, you could give that exact amount to a single parent who may not otherwise be able to pay for his or her child to attend.

Wisdom/Insight

Experience/Expertise

Time

Resources (such as a car, temporary housing, or a business suit for a job interview)

Money

LOVE CHALLENGE

Think of one specific gift that God has given you. How will you use that gift this week to give back to Him or to help someone else experience His love?

Use this space for more notes, quotes, or lessons learned from the chapter.

OBJECTIVE

In reading this chapter, you will learn how God uses acts of service
to communicate His love to and build relationships with people whose
primary love language is acts of service—and how those people can, in turn,
show love to others by performing meaningful service projects for them.

GOD SPEAKS LOVE LANGUAGE #4: ACTS OF SERVICE

INSTRUCTIONS: Complete this fifth lesson after reading chapter 5 ("God Speaks Love Language #4: Acts of Service," pp. 79–90) of *God Speaks Your Love Language.*

KEY TERM

Acts of service: a love language through which people experience emotional wholeness when chores or tasks are done for their benefit.

OPENING QUESTIONS

1. What were your household responsibilities when you were a kid? Which chores were tolerable, and which ones did you absolutely dread? Explain. What are your favorite and least favorite household chores today? Explain.

2. If you were facing a long day of chores, what would be the most helpful thing someone could do for you? What act of assistance would make the biggest impact? What would be your reaction if someone performed that act of service for you?

THINK ABOUT IT

3. Dr. Chapman begins the chapter with the inspiring story of Paul Brown, a teacher who goes far above the call of duty. Dr. Chapman states emphatically, **"Paul's primary love language is acts of service."** How does Paul Brown use acts of service to communicate love to others? Who benefits from his acts of service?

4. Dr. Chapman points out that Paul **"has made some sacrificial choices"** so that he can perform his acts of service. What are some of those sacrificial choices? What impact have his acts of service had on his life?

5. Dr. Chapman also shares the story of Mother Teresa, whose acts of service inspired the world. In pursuing her love language, Mother Teresa said, **"I had to do it. It was a calling. I knew I had to go; I did not know how to get there."** Where did she start? Dr. Chapman writes, **"She had no master blueprint for her work, but her goal was clear."** What was her goal? What acts of service did she perform to accomplish her goal?

6. What was the central message of Mother Teresa's life? How did she express the spiritual nature of her acts of service? Why was she so willing to embrace the sacrifices that came with her acts of service?

7. How did God express His love for humankind through acts of service? How did Jesus use His acts of service as evidence of the truthfulness of His claims?

8. Dr. Chapman writes, **"We can say that Jesus' entire life was an act of service."** What examples of service can we find in the Gospels? How did Jesus frame His own death as an act of service?

9. Dr. Chapman says, **"For all who examine the life of Jesus, He becomes a fork in the road of life."** What path do many people choose? What causes many of those people to choose that path? What does serving a God who speaks through acts of service motivate them to do?

TAKE IT HOME

Mother Teresa pointed out that people's perspectives change when they learn to see Christ in other people. Look at the following list of people. In the second column, describe how people might view and react to that person under typical circumstances. In the third column, describe how people might view and react to the person if they were able to see Christ in him or her.

PERSON	REACTION UNDER TYPICAL CIRCUMSTANCES	REACTION IF YOU SAW CHRIST IN THAT PERSON
An overbearing boss		
An acquaintance whose political views offend you		
A sibling struggling with an addiction		

FINDING TIME FOR SERVICE

Dr. Chapman points out that acts of service require sacrifice, starting with our time. The key to success, then, is finding the time. The first pair of clock faces below represent a typical day for you, a.m. and p.m. Divide them as you would a pie chart to show how you spend the hours of a typical day. The more specific you can be, the better. How many hours do you spend working? Sleeping? Eating? Exercising? Scrolling through social media?

For the second pair of clock faces, think about what a day might look like if you set aside time for acts of service. What areas could be scaled back—sacrificed—to make time to help others?

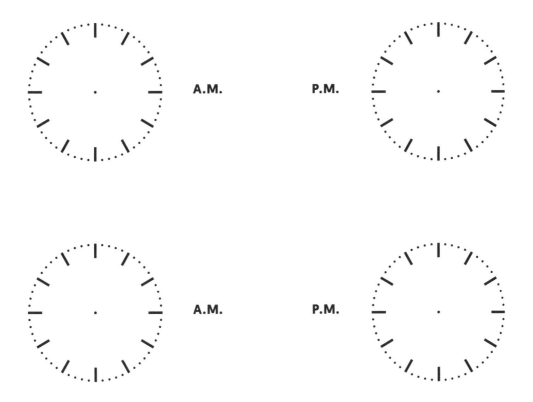

A.M.   P.M.

A.M.   P.M.

LOVE CHALLENGE

Think of one specific act of service that God has done for you. How will you express your gratitude for it? How will you celebrate its impact on your life? How will you make other people aware of His act of service? What act of service will you perform for someone else?

Use this space for more notes, quotes, or lessons learned from the chapter.

OBJECTIVE

In reading this chapter, you will learn how God uses physical touch to communicate His love to and build relationships with people whose primary love language is physical touch—and how those people can, in turn, show love to others by being purposeful in giving them meaningful physical contact.

GOD SPEAKS LOVE LANGUAGE #5: PHYSICAL TOUCH

INSTRUCTIONS: Complete this sixth lesson after reading chapter 6 ("God Speaks Love Language #5: Physical Touch," pp. 91–107) of *God Speaks Your Love Language.*

KEY TERM

Physical touch: a love language through which people experience emotional wholeness by way of physical contact.

OPENING QUESTIONS

1. What are the most memorable physical touches you've ever experienced? Maybe it was a high five from your favorite athlete. Or your first kiss. Or holding the hand of a grandparent in a hospital bed. Or a bear hug from your mom the first time you came home from college. Or your spouse feeling your forehead to check for a fever when you were sick. List as many memorable touches as you can recall.

2. If someone offered you $50 to go an entire day without touching anyone, would you do it? What about $500 to go an entire week without touching? Or $5,000 for an entire month? What would be your limit for going without physical touch? Why? If you did try to go a month, a week, or even a day without touching, what would be your biggest challenge? Why?

THINK ABOUT IT

3. Dr. Chapman writes, **"People whose primary love language is physical touch often speak of 'feeling the presence of God.'"** How did Karl, Dr. Chapman's German interpreter, experience the presence of God? How did Kevin, Greta's husband, experience the presence of God? How did the praise singers in Singapore experience the presence of God? What do these different encounters reveal about God?

4. Dr. Chapman talks about his encounter with Nicholas, a member of an inner-city house church. What experiences in Nicholas's past might explain why physical touch speaks so powerfully to him? What evidence did Dr. Chapman see of God's use of physical touch in His relationship with Nicholas?

5. **"Evidence that God speaks the love language of physical touch is seen throughout the Bible—both Old Testament and New Testament."** With these words of Dr. Chapman in mind, how did Jacob experience God's physical touch? How might Jacob's experience give hope to people today who are facing uncertainty?

6. Dr. Chapman writes, **"The biblical account of the life of Jesus shows that He frequently used physical touch as a love language."** Give some examples of how Jesus used physical touch during His ministry.

7. **"One of Jesus' most profound instances of using physical touch to convey love took place during His last supper with the disciples."** What were the circumstances? What did Jesus do to convey His love for His disciples through physical touch (and acts of service)? Why was His choice of expression especially powerful and unexpected? What did Jesus want His disciples to take away from the experience?

8. After Jesus returned to His Father, how did His followers continue His ministry of showing love to others through physical touch? How did Peter direct the praise and glory for his physical touch ministry back to Jesus, where it rightly belonged? What is the takeaway for believers today who show love to others through physical touch?

9. Dr. Chapman points out that **the greatest skeptics become the greatest believers when they personally experience God's touch.** Why are some people skeptical when others claim to have been "touched by God"? What does the story of Saul of Tarsus teach us about such skepticism?

TAKE IT HOME

How often do you use purposeful touch to communicate affection, friendliness, support, joy, or love? For each of the categories below, write an estimate of how many times you purposefully use that form of physical touch in an average week.

_____ Kisses

_____ Hugs

_____ Handshakes

_____ High fives

_____ Fist bumps

_____ Playful wrestling

_____ Shoulder massages

_____ Other: _____

THE POWER OF PHYSICAL TOUCH

God shows His love to us through physical touch and encourages us to do the same for others. How could you use physical touch to communicate God's love to the following people?

A church member mourning the loss of a loved one

A homeless person on your route to work

A young person who's being bullied

A coworker who's celebrating a promotion

A family who just moved to your neighborhood

A friend with whom you just had a disagreement

LOVE CHALLENGE

The story of Saul and Ananias in the book of Acts offers a powerful reminder of the life-changing potential of physical touch. With that in mind, what changes will you make to your daily routine this week to express love to others through physical touch?

Use this space for more notes, quotes, or lessons learned from the chapter.

OBJECTIVE

In reading this chapter, you will learn how knowing your
primary love language can deepen your relationship with God
and transform the way you experience His love in your daily life.

DISCOVERING YOUR PRIMARY LOVE LANGUAGE

INSTRUCTIONS: Complete this seventh lesson after reading chapter 7 ("Discovering Your Primary Love Language," pp. 109–129) of *God Speaks Your Love Language.*

KEY TERM

Primary love language: the method of communicating and experiencing emotional love that most profoundly impacts a person and causes him or her to feel truly loved.

In-love experience: a euphoric emotional obsession in which a person fixates on the positive aspects of a romantic partner—and of the relationship—but loses sight of practical realities.

OPENING QUESTIONS

1. Dr. Chapman tells the story of Matt, a farmer, who took his wife, Justine, for a plane ride so that she could see the words "I love you, Justine" that he had double-seeded in his wheat field. With that in mind, what's the most memorable expression of love anyone has ever shown you? What were the circumstances? What made it so special? How did you react?

2. You don't have to be friends with a pilot to pull off a grand romantic gesture. What is the most elaborate expression of love you've ever given someone? What were the circumstances? What made it so special? What kind of reaction did you get? In hindsight, what, if anything, would you have done differently?

THINK ABOUT IT

3. **"Couples can sincerely love each other, yet not connect emotionally."** What does Dr. Chapman identify as the problem in that situation? What happens if someone in a relationship simply does what comes naturally in expressing love to his or her partner? What happens if that expression of love doesn't align with the partner's primary love language?

4. **"The same tendency is true when it comes to receiving and reciprocating God's love."** In terms of love languages, how do most people tend to express their love for God? What does that expression look like in your life?

5. What three questions can help you discover your primary love language in human relationships? How would you answer each one? Based on your responses, what is your primary love language in human relationships? Do you think your closest friends and loved ones would agree? Explain.

6. What is the connection between your primary love language in human relationships and your preferred method of interacting with God? How would you answer the previous three questions in terms of your relationship with God?

7. In what two ways does understanding your primary love language affect your relationships with God and others? What do Dave, Beth, and John each understand about themselves? How does John's experience with his wife underscore the importance of understanding other believers' primary love language? What is your best strategy for understanding other believers' primary love language?

8. Dr. Chapman talks about his encounter with a man named Bill at a craft shop on the Blue Ridge Parkway. Bill talked about visiting his brother-in-law's church. What was his initial reaction to the worship experience there? How did learning the concept of love languages change Bill's attitude toward his brother-in-law? How did it change his brother-in-law's attitude toward his wife?

9. Dr. Chapman writes, **"As we explore our own love language, we need to remember that simply knowing that language won't protect us from suffering."** What is it especially important to remember during those times?

TAKE IT HOME

For each of the following categories, write down how old you were when you first discovered it and how the discovery impacted your life.

_____ Your favorite food

_____ Your favorite subject in school

_____ Your most impressive talent or skill

_____ Your best friend

_____ Your spiritual gift

_____ Your career path

_____ Your primary love language

EXPLAINING YOUR LOVE LANGUAGE

Dr. Chapman emphasizes the importance of interacting with God using different love languages. That presents us with the challenge—and opportunity—of learning other languages. Answer the following questions about your primary love language to help someone else who might be trying to learn it.

What makes you feel especially close to—and especially loved by—God?

What challenges do you face when it comes to communicating with God in your primary love language?

How do other people react to your preferred methods for getting close to God and experiencing His love?

How do you avoid questioning or being critical of another person's love language, especially in terms of his or her relationship with God?

LOVE CHALLENGE

Bill realized that he had misjudged his brother-in-law because he failed to recognize his brother-in-law's primary love language. When have you misjudged someone because you didn't understand his or her primary love language? What can you do this week to make amends—and to learn that love language?

Use this space for more notes, quotes, or lessons learned from the chapter.

OBJECTIVE

In reading this chapter, you will learn how to address the dullness or routine of your love language and discover new dialects that will allow you to communicate your love for God in new and exciting ways.

LEARNING TO SPEAK NEW DIALECTS OF LOVE

INSTRUCTIONS: Complete this eighth lesson after reading chapter 8 ("Learning to Speak New Dialects of Love," pp. 131–162) of *God Speaks Your Love Language*.

KEY TERM

Dialects: nuances within a love language that communicate love in more specific and powerful ways.

OPENING QUESTIONS

1. In your circle of acquaintances, how many different regional dialects do you hear spoken on a regular basis? Which dialects are the easiest to detect? Why? Which ones are more subtle?

2. What dialects, speech patterns, common phrases, and other conversational tendencies make your verbal communication unique? If someone were to imitate the way you speak, what would they do?

THINK ABOUT IT

3. Dr. Chapman points out, **"We are creatures of habit. From the time we rise in the morning, we tend to go through the same routines day after day."** What daily routines do you tend to follow? Why? How often do you feel the need to break out of your daily routine? What do you do when you feel that need?

4. Dr. Chapman goes on to say, **"Variety stimulates the mind and creativity livens up what could be a life of monotonous routine. I would like to suggest that the same principle applies to a love relationship with God. If we do only what comes naturally and express love to God in our usual manner, it is possible that even a relationship with God will become routine."** What routines tend to creep into your relationship with God if you're not careful?

5. On a scale of one to ten, with one being "utterly unpredictable" and ten being "perfectly predictable," how routine are your prayers of thanksgiving to God for His blessings in your life? What would your typical prayer of thanksgiving include? What would your prayer include if you focused on being less predictable with your words of affirmation?

6. What does quality time with God look like in your life? What similarities and differences do you see between the way you engage in quiet time with God and the ways Karen, Patrick, Julia, and Robert experience their time with God? How would printed resources or active movement enhance your quality time with God? What effect would extending the time you spend with God have on your relationship with Him? How would beginning and ending your day with God enhance your relationship with Him?

7. Dr. Chapman acknowledges that **"monetary gifts are common and are a logical starting point as a dialect for the love language of giving."** How did the young couple who had been married for six months and Jan and Mike speak their own dialects in giving money? What would speaking the dialect of meeting the physical needs of others look like in your life? What would the dialect of giving encouragement look like?

8. **"People whose primary love language is acts of service use whatever skills they have to do the work of God."** List several different skills that could be used for acts of service. What do you take away from the experiences of Carl, Maria, and Mark? If you were to focus on a specific dialect of the acts of service love language, what would it be? Explain.

9. Who are the **"untouchables"** in our society? What would it mean to them to have someone initiate purposeful, meaningful physical touch with them? What opportunities for physical touch did Kate and her daughter find in their local assisted-living complex?

TAKE IT HOME

Dr. Chapman emphasizes that each of us has a primary love language—a way of communicating love to God that we use more often than any other. Beyond that, we have varying degrees of comfort with and skill in using the other love languages. Take a moment to assess your strengths and weaknesses when it comes to using each love language to deepen your relationship with God. For example, you may list "a lack of resources" as a weakness when it comes to gifts.

LOVE LANGUAGE	STRENGTHS	WEAKNESSES
Words of Affirmation		
Quality Time		
Gifts		
Acts of Service		
Physical Touch		

FIVE NEW DIALECTS

Dialects allow you to connect with God in especially meaningful ways. Learning new dialects can be challenging, but the results are worth the effort. For each love language, think of a specific dialect you could learn that would help you experience God's love—or express your love for Him—in an especially powerful way. For example, by mastering a few basic home design/handyman skills, you could perform the act of service of creating a prayer/Bible study nook in your home.

WORDS OF AFFIRMATION

QUALITY TIME

GIFTS

ACTS OF SERVICE

PHYSICAL TOUCH

LOVE CHALLENGE

Remember: you don't have to fully master a dialect before you put it to use. With that in mind, what new dialect will you use to deepen your relationship with God this week?

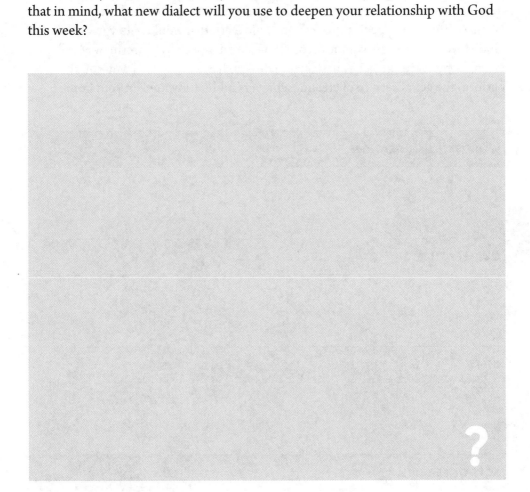

Use this space for more notes, quotes, or lessons learned from the chapter.

OBJECTIVE

In reading this chapter, you will discover how learning to communicate
with God in a new love language can deepen your relationship with Him.

GETTING OUT OF YOUR COMFORT ZONE

9

INSTRUCTIONS: Complete this ninth lesson after reading chapter 9 ("Getting Out of Your Comfort Zone," pp. 163–178) of *God Speaks Your Love Language*.

KEY TERM

Comfort zone: an environment in which a person feels most at ease or a behavior pattern that comes naturally to a person.

OPENING QUESTIONS

1. What is your comfort zone in a social setting? Do you prefer noisy, crowded parties or small, quiet gatherings with a few friends? Do you prefer the company of interesting acquaintances and strangers or of familiar and predictable friends? Do you prefer to be active or sedate when you socialize? Explain.

2. What is your comfort zone in a work setting? Do you prefer an office atmosphere or a remote worksite? Do you prefer to work as part of a team or to work alone? Are you more productive in a traditional forty-hour, nine-to-five, Monday-through-Friday schedule, or are you more productive when you can set your own hours? Do you prefer business attire, business casual, or ultra-casual? Explain.

THINK ABOUT IT

3.   When was the last time you stepped out of your comfort zone, whether in a social setting, a work setting, or a spiritual setting? What prompted you to change up your routine? What did you do? Were you satisfied with the results? Explain.

4.   Learning to speak a new love language certainly qualifies as stepping outside your comfort zone. What challenges can you expect to face as you learn to show your love for God in a new way? How do your efforts honor Him?

5.   Dr. Chapman says, **"I think God is super delighted when He sees you seeking to speak your love in a language that is new to you."** Based on Dr. Chapman's personal experience, what happens when you learn to love God in languages that are not comfortable to you?

6.   What was Karen's first reaction to her friend's suggestion that she join a medical missions trip to Africa? What changed her mind? What happened when she stepped outside her comfort zone and started speaking the love language of acts of service?

7. What was Ron's comfort zone in his Christian service? What caused him to start looking beyond his comfort zone in his relationship with God? What was the first step he took in learning to speak the love language of quality time? What challenge did he face? What steps did he take to overcome the challenge?

8. What is Monique's primary love language? What dialects did she use in speaking her primary love language with God? What made her aware of the need to learn a new love language? What were her first steps in learning to speak the love language of physical touch? How did she use her new love language to reach out to others on God's behalf?

9. How did Tom speak his primary love language, physical touch, in his daily interaction with others? How did he speak it in his interaction with God? What caused Tom to consider learning a new love language? What steps did he take to begin speaking the love language of gifts?

TAKE IT HOME

Use the following chart to explore your comfort zone when it comes to expressing your love for God. In the center circle, identify the dialect you're most comfortable with. For example, if your primary love language is words of affirmation, you may be most comfortable with singing hymns and praise songs. In the next ring, identify a dialect or love language that's slightly less comfortable for you. Keep going until you get to the outer ring, which should be a dialect or love language that's way out of your comfort zone.

HOW TO STEP OUTSIDE YOUR COMFORT ZONE

In this chapter, Dr. Chapman talks about four people who rejuvenated their relationship with God by learning to speak a new love language. Their experiences offer helpful snapshots for others who are interested in doing the same.

Of the four people, which one do you most closely identify with? Explain.

Which new love language are you most interested in learning? Explain.

What's the best-case scenario for learning that language? How will it impact your relationship with God?

What's the biggest challenge you'll face in learning the new love language?

LOVE CHALLENGE

On the "How to Step Outside Your Comfort Zone" sheet, you identified a new love language you would be interested in learning. What steps will you take this week to begin learning that love language?

STEP 1

STEP 2

STEP 3

STEP 4

STEP 5

STEP 6

Use this space for more notes, quotes, or lessons learned from the chapter.

OBJECTIVE

In reading this chapter, you will learn how to love others in a
difference-making way as a response to God's first loving you
and graciously accepting you into His family.

WHATEVER THE LANGUAGE, LET LOVE PREVAIL

10

INSTRUCTIONS: Complete this tenth lesson after reading chapter 10 ("Whatever the Language, Let Love Prevail," pp. 179–193) of *God Speaks Your Love Language.*

KEY TERM

Multilingual: able to communicate love effectively in all five love languages.

OPENING QUESTIONS

1. List as many Bible passages, song lyrics, movie quotes, lines of poetry, or familiar sayings you can think of that describe what love is—or isn't. Which ones hit closest to home for you? Which ones have shaped your views of love? Explain.

2. Anyone can say the words "I love you." How can you tell the difference between someone who's speaking those words from the heart and someone who's saying them with an ulterior motive? What actions would convince you that a person's love for you is sincere?

THINK ABOUT IT

3. Dr. Chapman explains that because people are estranged from God, our natural instinct regarding love is somewhat skewed. In our natural state, who do we tend to love? What is the **"rule of the day"** for individuals as well as many of the world's religions? What was Jesus' radical teaching when it came to loving others?

4. Dr. Chapman writes, **"The question is how to break free from the earthbound weight of human love to experience the freedom of divine love."** Where does the answer to this dilemma lie?

5. What was the "new command" that Jesus gave His disciples? What role did love play in identifying Jesus' followers?

6. Dr. Chapman writes, **"We come to God as individuals, but once the God connection is made, He places us into His family."** What does that family connection guarantee for believers for the rest of our lives? What responsibility does it give us toward people who are not yet part of God's family?

7. **"Whatever love language God speaks to draw us to Him will be the love language we most naturally use to express our love to God. But we must not stop there."** How did the apostle Paul explain the next step? Learning one love language is challenging enough. Learning two—let alone all five—seems like a lot to ask. Why is it essential to remember that the One who is asking this of us "is able to do immeasurably more than all we ask or imagine" (Ephesians 3:20)?

8. Dr. Chapman reminds us, **"We do not love others in order to be accepted by God; we love them in response to God's first loving us and graciously accepting us into His family."** How does learning to communicate in all five love languages enhance our usefulness in the community of God? What will happen when love prevails in the Christian community?

9. Dr. Chapman concludes the chapter by pointing to the greatest expression of love in human history: the sacrificial death of Jesus. He writes, **"The cross has become the universal symbol of God's love. The crucifixion of Jesus was a time when God clearly spoke all five love languages."** What words of affirmation did Jesus speak from the cross? What act of service did He perform in His death? What gift did His sacrifice make possible? How did He make quality time with God possible? How did God touch humanity through the death of His Son?

TAKE IT HOME

Think of some of the differences between human love and God's love and list them below. For example, human love extends to the people closest to us—usually family members and cherished friends. God's love extends to everyone, including enemies. Human love often ebbs and flows, depending on our circumstances and moods. God's love is constant.

HUMAN LOVE	GOD'S LOVE

What makes it possible for us to show God's love to others?

LOVE IN ACTION

Dr. Chapman doesn't claim that showing God's love to others will be easy. In fact, he's very clear about the sacrifices involved. Yet God uses those sacrifices to effect powerful changes—not only in the lives of the people we love, but in our own lives as well. For each of the following people, describe the challenge of showing God's love to that person and then offer some ideas for overcoming the challenge.

A coworker who, politically speaking, represents everything you oppose

The Challenge   Ideas for Overcoming the Challenge

The parent of a child who's been bullying your child

The Challenge   Ideas for Overcoming the Challenge

A mentally ill family member

The Challenge   Ideas for Overcoming the Challenge

LOVE CHALLENGE

Dr. Chapman tells the story of Nicky Cruz's dramatic transformation from drug-addicted gang leader to follower of Christ—a transformation that was fostered by the loving, courageous outreach of David Wilkerson. Dr. Chapman offers a simple yet powerful summary of their encounter: **"Love prevails."** With that in mind, what loving—and perhaps courageous—step can you take this week to allow God's love to prevail in someone else's life?

Use this space for more notes, quotes, or lessons learned from the chapter.

GOD SPEAKS YOUR LOVE LANGUAGE LEADER'S GUIDE

Congratulations! You're on the cusp of an exciting adventure. You're about to lead a small group through ten studies that will enrich relationships and change lives. And you'll have a front-row seat to it all.

You'll find that every small group presents its own unique challenges and opportunities. But there are some tips that can help you get the most out of any small-group study, whether you're a seasoned veteran or a first-time leader.

1. Communicate.

From the outset, you'll want to give members a sense of how your group dynamic will work. To maximize your time together, group members will need to read each lesson's assigned chapter of *God Speaks Your Love Language* and then complete the "Opening Questions" (questions 1–2) and "Think about It" section (questions 3–9) *before* the meeting. The "Take It Home" and "Love Challenge" activities should be completed after the meeting.

2. Keep a good pace.

Your first meeting will begin with introductions (if necessary). After that, you'll ask group members to share their responses to the first two "Opening Questions." These are icebreakers. Their purpose is merely to introduce the session topic. You'll want to give everyone a chance to share, but you don't want to get sidetracked by overly long discussions here.

The "Think about It" section (questions 3–9) is the heart of the study. This is where most of your discussion should occur. You'll need to establish a good pace, making sure that you give each question its due while allowing enough time to tackle all of them. After you've finished your discussion of the questions, briefly go over the "Take It Home" and "Love Challenge" sections so that group members know what their "homework" will be.

Your next meeting will begin with a brief review of that homework. Ask volunteers to share their responses to the "Take It Home" activities and their experiences in implementing the "Love Challenge." After about five minutes of reviewing your group members' application of the previous lesson, begin your new lesson.

3. Prepare.

Read each chapter, answer the study questions, and work through the take-home material, just like your group members will do. Try to anticipate questions or comments your group members will have. If you have time, think of stories from your own experience or from the experiences of people you know that apply to the lesson. That way, if you have a lull during your study, you can use the stories to spark conversation.

4. Be open and vulnerable.

Not everyone is comfortable sharing the details of their relationship with God with other people. Yet openness and vulnerability are essential in a group setting. That's where you come in. If you have the courage to be vulnerable, to share less-than-flattering details about your own relationship with Him, you may give others the courage to do the same.

5. Emphasize and celebrate the uniqueness of every follower of God.

Some group members may feel intimidated by other people's seemingly successful relationship with God. Others may find that strategies for learning love languages that work for some people don't work for them—and they may get discouraged. You can head off that discouragement by opening up about your own struggles and successes. Help group members see that, beneath the surface, every follower of God faces challenges.

6. Create a safe haven where people feel free—and comfortable—to share.

Ask group members to agree to some guidelines before your first meeting. For example, what is said in the group setting stays in the group setting. And every person's voice deserves to be heard. If you find that some group members are quick to give unsolicited advice or criticism when other people share, remind the group that every person's situation is unique. What works for one may not work for another. If the problem persists, talk with your advice givers and critics one-on-one. Help them see how their well-intended comments may be having the unintended effect of discouraging others from talking.

7. Follow up.

The questions and activities in this book encourage group members to incorporate new strategies in their spiritual lives and make significant changes to their relationships with God and others. You can be the cheerleader your group members need by celebrating their successes and congratulating them for their courage and commitment. Also, by checking in each week with your group members, you create accountability and give them motivation to apply the *God Speaks Your Love Language* principles to their lives.

Every marriage is a growing marriage. The real question is: Are you growing *closer together* or *further apart*?

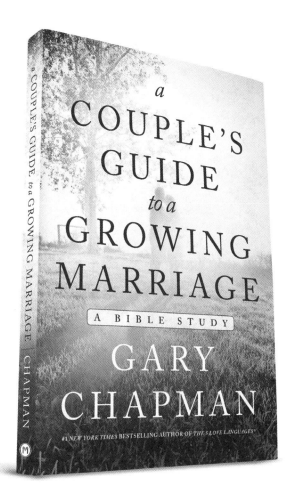

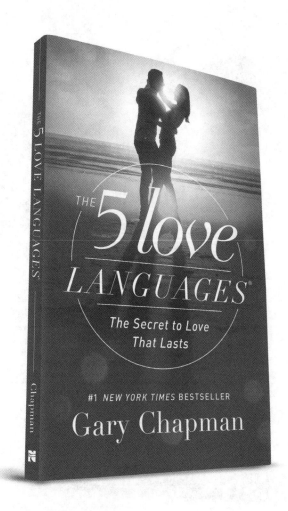

LOVE + HOPE SERIES

Finding Strength, Gaining Courage—One Language At a Time

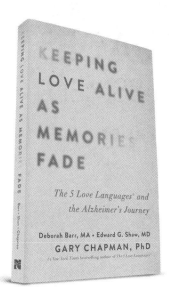

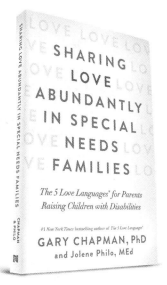

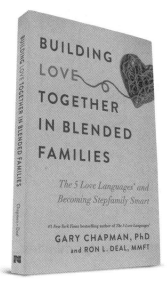

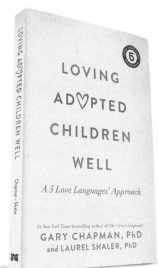

NORTHFIELD
PUBLISHING

THE FIVE LOVE LANGUAGES®
FOR LIFE'S UNEXPECTED CIRCUMSTANCES

Also available as eBooks and audiobooks